## CONTENTS



ISBN 978-1-4234-5867-8

7777 W. Bluemound Rd. P.O. Box 13819 Milwaukee, WI 53213

# IN THE BEGINNING - CELTIC THUNDER

BY PHIL COULTER

This may very well be the oddest collection of songs ever gathered together in one folio!

How can a rock anthem like 'I Want to Know What Love Is' sit comfortably beside an Irish folk song like 'Raggle Taggle Gypsy' or the cheesiest of pop classics 'Puppy Love' share the same space as the supremely tender 'The Old Man'? The answer is Celtic Thunder.

This is a show which defies musical pigeon-holing and effortlessly moves through a whole range of genres. But this is the important thing. The songs may source from very different backgrounds but they all have one thing in common. They are all great songs. They all have a strong melody, a well crafted lyric and a spark that connects with people.

THIS IS A SHOW WHICH DEFIES MUSICAL PIGEON-HOLING AND EFFORTLESSLY MOVES THROUGH A WHOLE RANGE OF GENRES

The curious thing about the evolution of Celtic Thunder is that the songs did not come first.

First came the concept - a television special that would celebrate in music the complex character of the Celtic male - at times sensitive, at others roguish, at times flirtatious, at others vulnerable ... but always manly.

Then came the casting, through a series of open auditions in Ireland and Scotland. Long hours in draughty rehearsal rooms paid off and produced the goods - five unknowns aged from fourteen to forty. Strong individuals from different backgrounds, each with this own voice and his own story to tell but each with a passion for singing and a hunger for the chance to go for it.

# Celtic Thunder

Damien McGinty (14) was still at school with the charm of the kid next door and the confidence of a veteran. When he twinkled those baby blues, opened his throat and let out this huge voice, it was game over!

Keith Harkin (21), who nearly missed the audition because, as usual, his mind was on more important things - like surfing and girls. He ambled in carrying a beat-up guitar and casually started tuning it as he was still talking. Simply a natural, before he'd even finished his first song he was signed up.

STRONG INDIVIDUALS FROM DIFFERENT BACKGROUNDS, EACH WITH THIS OWN VOICE AND HIS OWN STORY TO TELL

Paul Byrom (28) the only singer with any vocal training or professional experience in the music business. Very much today's idea of an Irish Tenor, his glorious voice coupled with dashing good looks and a glint in his eye, made him an easy choice.

George Donaldson (40) had been a semi-professional folk singer in Scotland for twenty years and was convinced that the big break was never going to come his way. His sincerity, his maturity and his old fashioned likability, coupled with a warm story-telling voice, combined to give him that chance.

Ryan Kelly (26), with the classic Irish looks. A super intelligent University graduate, then working in banking, Ryan was almost too nice at the auditions until he sang a Judas song from Jesus Christ Superstar and immediately became 'The Dark Destroyer.'

Then came the tough job of finding, or writing, the songs that would fit each of the performers' personalities and build the framework of the show. No easy task!

# THE VISION OF CELTIC THUNDER

SHARON BROWNE - PRODUCER

The concept for Celtic Thunder was to create a show featuring Real Men of different ages from Ireland and Scotland. A range of Celts! There are enough 'boybands' out there, it is time for some REAL MEN.

Damien, Keith, Paul, Ryan and George are all individual talents, each with a specific type of voice and their own distinct personality, character and style of performance. Celtic Thunder brings them together to celebrate this range of unique talents and also treat audiences to powerful ensemble pieces where the diversity and range of these performances are captured.

SONGS THAT REKINDLE MEMORIES OF HOPE, LOVE AND LOSS. SONGS THAT REFLECT AMBITION, COMPETITION AND UNITY.

Celtic Thunder - the show, is not just about the music. The eclectic mix of songs in Celtic Thunder is there to show diversity. Each singer has his own selection of songs to perform, written or chosen specifically to suit his style of singing and his own distinct personality. The ensemble numbers are designed to reflect the power of these men's

voices combined in songs that celebrate their Celtic heritage, be it Scottish or Irish. Performing these songs together, uniting Celts the world over who share this common heritage, makes the experience particularly special.

All of these men, even the little man, are Celtic. Phil Coulter, legendary songwriter and composer is Celtic. Creator and producer, Sharon Browne, is Celtic. The songs are a mix of Celtic Songs and Classic Songs performed by Celtic Men.

LYRICS THAT STRIKE AN EMOTIVE NOTE AND BIG POWERFUL BALLADS TO REFLECT AND CELEBRATE MANLINESS.

The aim of the music and songs in the show is to strike a chord with each and every person in the audience. Songs that rekindle memories of hope, love and loss. Songs that reflect ambition, competition and unity. Songs with meaningful lyrics that strike an emotive note and big powerful ballads to reflect and celebrate manliness.

Celtic Thunder is a portrayal of men in music, all men, celebrating men's individuality, power and strength.

# THE SONGS

**HEARTLAND** the powerful and dramatic opening was specially composed by PHIL COULTER. The smouldering overture, combining the sound of real thunder, creaking ship's timbers and mournful Irish pipes sets the mood for the show. As the mist clears, we see a rocky shore line, dominated by the battered sail and broken hulk of a shipwreck, heightening the sense of expectation, of an arrival. The first words we hear are intoned by a haunting figure whose image appears on the sail,

> "Out of the mists of time, it comes,
> Older than the oldest rhyme, it comes
> Coursing through our veins, it comes
> Pulsing in our brains, it comes
> Crashing like a thunder roll,
> Echoing in our very soul,
> Listen for it as it comes

The pure and primal sound.... of drums!
As the hypnotic rhythm pattern builds through the orchestra we see the shadowy figures of six monks as they move across the set singing in plainchant an ancient prayer in Greek - "Kyrie eleison, Christe eleison" - Lord have mercy, Christ have mercy." This theme is taken up in the chorus of the song, now sung in Gaelic, "A Thiarna Dean Trocaire, A Chriost Dean Trocaire" - Lord have mercy, Christ have mercy.

**THE MOUNTAINS OF MOURNE** is one of the most popular of Irish songs. The words were written in 1896 by the prolific and multi-talented Percy French to an old Irish air. Among the many recorded versions of the song was one by American singer/songwriter Don McClean. Our own troubadour KEITH HARKIN puts his own stamp on the song.

**RAGGLE TAGGLE GYPSY** This theme of the lady running off with a gypsy lover is found in many folk songs, from the Gaelic 'An Spailpin Fanach' to 'Gypsy Davy' recorded by American folk icons like Woody Guthrie and Pete Seeger. One of the first recordings of this particular version was in 1973 by the seminal Irish band PLANXTY. In Celtic Thunder it becomes a vehicle for a stand-off between three percussionists.

**RIDE ON** was written by one of Ireland's leading songwriters JIMMY MCCARTHY, who was a jockey in a previous life,hence the ease of his use of images to do with the horse. Originally recorded by CHRISTY MOORE, the song has become a staple in Irish folk music, though this version, by RYAN KELLY is a lot more rocky!

**COME BY THE HILLS/BUACHAILL O'N EIRNE.** One of the most gorgeous of Irish folk songs, Buachaill O'n Eirne, meaning "I am a lad from the banks of the Erne," has long been a favourite with many different versions recorded, even orchestrally. The English words were added by Scots singer Gordon Smith. It is perfectly suited to DAMIEN'S young voice.

**THE OLD MAN** was written by PHIL COULTER and originally recorded by The Furey Brothers, when he ws producing the band in the early '80's. The song is regarded as a standard in Irish contemporary folk music and has been recorded by many leading lights, including Irish Tenor RONAN TYNAN and Canadian veteran JOHN McDERMOTT. GEORGE DONALDSON sings the song as if he reallty means it. And he does.

**LOVE THEE DEAREST.** Thomas Moore, one of Ireland's greatest poets, isprobably best known for lyrics written to collections of Irish traditional tunes called 'Moore's Melodies,' a series of which were published in the early 1800's. They included classics like 'The Last Rose of Summer,' 'The Minstrel Boy,' and 'Believe Me If All Those Endearing Young Charms.' For this particular version, Musical Director PHIL COULTER came up with the idea of singing two of the verses in Italian, to bring something fresh to this much loved and much performed song. He enlisted the help of fellow songwriters Frank Musker and Kaballah to come up with a beautifully resonant Italian lyric, delivered with great panache by PAUL BYROM.

**HEARTBREAKER** This is the song which defines the role of RYAN KELLY in the show, firmly casting him as 'The Dark Destroyer.' Specially written by PHIL COULTER, it has a very sexy tango feel and a rather sensuous cello solo.

**NIGHTS IN WHITE SATIN.** Possibly the most melodic of all the mega successful English rock bands to conquer America in the '60's were THE MOODY BLUES. This was the biggest of all their multi-million selling records. Written by JUSTIN HAYWARD, it truly is a pop classic which sounds just as fresh and every bit as powerful when sung in the show by PAUL BYROM.

**A BIRD WITHOUT WINGS.** One of the most requested songs in the show, it features an interplay between young Damien and the more mature George, to highlight that special bond between father and son. This song was written by PHIL COULTER and legendary music business veteran MIKE CHAPMAN, whose credits include the classic 'SIMPLY THE BEST.'

**THE VOYAGE** was written by a very gifted and much underrated Galway based singer/songwriter called JOHNNY DUHAN. A huge favourite at weddings in Ireland, it was originally recorded by CHRISTY MOORE. As GEORGE sang this at the filming, he could look out at the audience and see his wife and young daughter.

**THE ISLAND.** A contemporary and, by a strange quirk of fate, college classmate of Phil Coulter, PAUL BRADY is one of the leading lights in Irish songwriting, with songs recorded by a range of stars from Tina Turner to Brooks and Dunn. This song inspired by the troubles in his native Northern Ireland is one of his best. This version by KEITH HARKIN, who hails from Derry, is particularly emotive.

**BROTHERS IN ARMS.** This is the title track from one of the biggest selling albums of all time, recorded by the superb 'DIRE STRAITS.' The engine room in that band, as songwriter, vocalist and guitarist was the mighty MARK KNOPFLER. A fascinating side to this man is his passion for Celtic music, as demonstrated in another two of his compositions featured orchestrally in the show, CAL and LOCAL HERO.

**MULL OF KINTYRE.** After the demise of the Beatles, PAUL McCARTNEY re-merged with his new band WINGS and this was one of their biggest hits. The Scots 'campfire sing-along' feel made it a perfect choice as an ensemble piece for the show.

**PUPPY LOVE.** For people of a certain age this song immediately brings to mind Donny, the Osmonds and the whole teeny-bopper phenomenon. DAMIEN MCGINTY just revels in the song. Eat your heart out, Donny.

**LAUREN AND I.** Before being signed for Celtic Thunder, KEITH HARKIN had been doing the rounds of the music pubs in his home town - just him and his guitar, learning the ropes and trying out his songs. His songwriting potential was soon spotted during early rehearsals, and there was no one more thrilled than Keith when one of his songs was chosen to be given the full treatment.

**STEAL AWAY.** Lots of people sing this song and believe it's a folk song from way-back-when. In fact it was written by PHIL COULTER, back in the '80's and has quietly found its way into peoples' hearts.

**REMEMBER ME (RECUERDAME).** This was originally composed by PHIL COULTER as an orchestral piece and recorded, with JAMES GALWAY, under the title 'Lament for the Wild Geese.' Since Phil wrote the lyrics, setting the song in the period of the Spanish Civil War, it has been recorded by more than a dozen singers but, according to the songwriter himself, this PAUL BYROM version is the best.

**MY BOY.** Yet another piece of work from the pen of PHIL COULTER. This song was originally recorded by the Irish actor RICHARD HARRIS, following on from his huge record success with 'McArthur Park.' It was subsequently picked up by The King, ELVIS PRESLEY, who took his version high in the U.S. charts. As a mature man, GEORGE DONALDSON delivers the song with great credibility.

**DESPERADO.** One of the great iconic songs of all time. The glorious combination of a wonderfully flowing melody and a lyric that is pure Americana, bathed in the sumptuous vocal harmonies of The Eagles guaranteed this song's place in the Pantheon of popular music. It's for sure that they would approve of this reading by RYAN KELLY.

**IRELAND'S CALL.** When the powers-that-be in Rugby Football in Ireland felt that they needed a sporting anthem that would inspire players and fans, respecting the fact that they came from both communities, North and South, the man they called in was PHIL COULTER. At international matches the song can be heard being sung at full volume by up to 50,000 people. Inspiring indeed.

**THAT'S A WOMAN.** Again specially written for the show by PHIL COULTER this song sets up a duel for a lady's affections between PAUL, the clean cut hero and RYAN, the Dark Destroyer. As is so often the case, the bad boy wins out! One critic reckoned that the song sounded as if it had been lifted from a hit Broadway musical!

**SHE** has an impressive pedigree. It was composed by the legendary French star CHARLES AZNAVOUR, with lyrics by HERBERT KRETZMER, whose other credits include the phenomenally successful stage musical LES MISERABLES. One of the stand-out versions recorde is by ELVIS COSTELLO. PAUL, having just been rejected, brings a nice vulnerability to the song.

**YOUNG LOVE.** Think TAB HUNTER and SONNY JAMES (whose versions of the song were both in the top three in the U.S. at the same time, back in 1957), and, much later, DONNY OSMOND. As DAMIEN proves in the show, this song has still got the magic.

**I WANT TO KNOW WHAT LOVE IS.** A huge hit on both sides of the Atlantic more than twenty years ago for FOREIGNER. This is one of the great rock anthems, crying out for a big orchestra, and every bit as powerful today as it ever was. KEITH just loved singing this.

**CAL/LOCAL HERO.** An orchestral arrangement of two film scores, composed by MARK KNOPFLER, this piece showcases the organic sound of the Irish pipes and whistles, and Knopfleresque guitar against a backdrop of soaring strings, wind and brass. Irresistible.

**CALEDONIA.** This spirited celebration of the power of the Celtic soul was written by Scots singer/songwriter DOUGIE McCLEAN. Harnessing the combined might of singers, orchestra and Highland pipes and Drums it is the perfect finale to Celtic Thunder.

**YESTERDAY'S MEN.** The '80's saw the beginning of the rapid advance in technology and the relocating of manufacturing to Third World countries with cheaper work forces. This led to the wholesale closure of traditional plants and factories and the decimation of the work force. PHIL COULTER wrote this song then and sadly it is still as relevant today.

# A BIRD WITHOUT WINGS

Words and Music by
PHIL COULTER and MIKE CHAPMAN

A
E
E7
A
D
I would - n't know what to do, I'd be lost with - out you watch - ing ov - er me.
A
A
E
I get so lone - ly when you're aw - ay.
D
A/E
E
I count ev - 'ry mom - ent,
I wait ev - 'ry day
A
D
un - til you're home ag - ain and hold me so tight:

A
E
A
D
A
that's when I know ev - 'ry - thing is all right.
Like a bird with - out
A
E
wings,
that longs to be fly - ing,
like a moth - er - less
D
A/E
E
child
left lone - ly and cry - ing;
like a song with - out
A
E/D
D
words,
like a world with - out mus - ic,
I would - n't know what to

A E E7 A D A
do, I'd be lost with - out you watch - ing ov - er me.
A E
You're my guard - ian ang-el, my light and my guide,
D A/E E
your hand on my shoulder - er and you by my side.
A D
You make ev - 'ry - thing beau - ti - ful, you make me comp - lete:

A E A D A
ev - 'ry - thing in my world, I'll lay at your feet. Like a church with no
D A
steep - le, where the bell nev - er rings, in a town with no
E A
peo - ple, where no voice in the choir ev - er sings! If a boat on the
D A
oc - ean would be lost with no sail, then, with - out your dev -

E
E7
A
ot - ion, sure - ly all that I dreamed of would fail!
F7
B♭
F
E♭
B♭/F
F
Like a song with - out

B♭
F/E♭
E♭
words,
like a world with-out mus - ic,
I would - n't know what to do, I'd be lost with - out you watch-ing ov - er
F
F7
me.
I would - n't know what to do, I'd be lost with - out
Molto rubato
you watch - ing ov - er me.

# CALEDONIA

Music and Lyrics by
DOUGIE MacLEAN

C/E F B♭ F
why I seem so far a - way to - day.
con - science fly - in' some - where in the wind.
Let me tell you that I
C/E F F/A B♭ F
love you and I think a - bout you all the time. Cal - ed - on - i - a, you're call - ing me, now I'm
C F F C/G F/A
go - in' home. But, if I should be - come a strang - er, know that it would make me more than
B♭ C 1 F B♭
sad: Cal - ed - on - i - a's been ev' - ry - thing I've ev - er had.

F
B♭
D m
B♭
F
E♭
had.
Bagpipes
B♭/D
E♭
A♭
E♭
B♭/D
E♭
E♭/G
A♭
E♭
B♭/D
E♭
E♭/G
A♭
Let me tell you that I love you and I think a - bout you all the time.

E♭
B♭
Cal - ed - on - i - a, you're call - ing me, now I'm go - in' home. But,
B♭/D
E♭
E♭/G
A♭
if I should be - come a strang - er, know that it would make me more than sad:
B♭
B♭
Cal - ed - on - i - a's been ev' - ry - thing I've ev - er
E♭
A♭
E♭
A♭
E♭
A♭
E♭
had.

# COME BY THE HILLS
## (Buachaill on Eirne)

Arranged by
PHIL COULTER

B
E
B
Corc - aigh da meid e, dha thaobh an ghlean-na, is Tir
F♯
B
E/B
Eoghain, is mu-ra n'a - thra me beas - ai, is me an t'oidhre ar
E/B
B
G
G Dm7 G
Chon - tae Mhuigh-eo.
C
F
C
F
C
Come by the hills to the land where fan-cy is free,
Come by the hills to the land where life is a song,

F
C
and stand where the peaks meet the sky and the loughs meet the
and stand where the birds fill the air with their joy all day
G/B
G
C
F
sea. Where the riv - ers run clear and the brack - en is
long; where the trees sway in time, and ev - en the
C
G
A m7
G/B
G
C
F
gold in the sun, and the cares of tom - or - row can
wind sings in tune, and the cares of tom - or - row can
C
F
C
1
wait till this day is done!
wait till this day is done.

2
C
F
C
Come by the hills to the land where
F
C
leg - end re - mains: the stor - ies of
F
C
G/B
old fill the heart and may yet come ag - ain.
G
C
F
Where the past has been lost, and the fut - ure has

C G G/B G C
still to be won, and the cares of tom -
F C F C
or - row can wait till this day is done. And the
F C F
cares of tom - or - row can wait till this day
C
is done!

# HEARTBREAKER

Words and Music by
PHIL COULTER

Tango

Em(add9) *mf*

Em(add9) Am(add9) D/F♯

They say that I'm a bad boy, that I just can't
They say I'm the dark dest - roy - er, that I just can't

G Em(add9) Am(add9)

help my - self, that, ev - en tho' I know I should,
get en - ough of girls hang - ing on a string,

B7♭9 Em

I'm just too bad to be good! They call me a rom -
that I'm on - ly af - ter one thing, that I'm filled with des -

Am(add9)
D/F♯
G
anc - er, a chanc - er, a gig - o - lo
ire, a li - ar, a rom - e - o!
Em(add9)
Am(add9)
B7♭9
who'll al - ways have an al - i - bi, who'll kiss the girls and
Like a bee in a hon - ey - comb, "Wel - come to the
Em
C
G
make them cry.
Pleas - ure Dome"!
I NEV - ER MEANT TO HURT YOU,
G
Em
I NEV - ER MEANT TO BREAK YOUR HEART IN TWO! I'M SOR - RY IF I

C G G Em
HURT ___ YOU; I'M SOR - RY, ___ BUT IT'S WHAT I SEEM ___ TO DO. ___
Em Am/G G G
— THEY CALL ME A HEART - BREAK - ER, NOTH - ING BUT A
Am/G G
HEART - BREAK - ER.
1 G B/F♯
2
Em(add9) Am(add9)

B7♭9
Em
Em
Am(add9)
I just can't live with - out it,
D/F♯
G
Em(add9)
the thrill of a wom - an's touch.
It's writ - ten in the
Am(add9)
B7♭9
Em
stars ab - ove;
I'm just ad - dict - ed to love.

Em
Am(add9)
D/F♯
But they all want to tame me, to chain me and
G
Em(add9)
Am(add9)
tie me down: don't they know I was born to be
B7♭9
Em
foot-loose and fan-cy free?
I NEV-ER MEANT TO
C
G
G
Em
HURT YOU, I NEV-ER MEANT TO BREAK YOUR HEART IN TWO!

C G G
I'M SOR-RY IF I HURT YOU; I'M SOR - RY, BUT IT'S
Em Em
WHAT I SEEM TO DO. THEY CALL ME A
Am/G G G
HEART - BREAK - ER, NOTH - ING BUT A
Am/G G F♯m7♭5 B7 Em
HEART - BREAK - ER.

# HEARTLAND

By PHIL COULTER

Bm
Bm
A/B
Bm
keep: shel - ter us and save us
roars, de - liv - er us from the oc - ean,
G
A
F♯
D
from the deep!
save our souls!
A THIAR - NA DEAN
G/D
D
G
D
D/A
A
TRO - CAIR-E, A CHRIOST DEAN TRO - CAIR - E A
D
G
D
G
D/A
A
D
THIAR - NA DEAN TRO - CAIR-E, A CHRIOST DEAN TRO - CAIR-E!

(Male vox - chant)
Bm A/B Bm G A Bm
Thank you, Lord, you have brought us safe to shore.
Bm A/B Bm G A F#
Be our strength and pro-tect-ion ev-er-more! A
D G/D D G D D/A A
THIAR-NA DEAN TRO-CAIR-E, A CHRIOST DEAN TRO-CAIR-E A

D G/D D G D/A A D
THIAR - NA DEAN TRO - CAIR - E, A CHRIOST DEAN TRO - CAIR - E! DEAN
A/C♯ D A/C♯ Bm Bm/A G G/F♯ Em Em/D A/C♯ A/B A
TRO - CAIR - E, DEAN TRO - CAIR - E, A THIAR - NA A
D G/D D G D
THIAR - NA DEAN TRO - CAIR - E, A CHRIOST DEAN
D/A A D G/D D
TRO - CAIR - E A THIAR - NA DEAN TRO - CAIR - E, A

G
D/A
A
D
CHRIOST
DEAN
TRO - CAIR - E!
E
A/E
E
TRO - CAIR - E,
A
A
E
E/B
B
E
CHRIOST
DEAN
TRO - CAIR - E
A
THIAR - NA
DEAN
A/E
E
A
E/B
B
E
TRO - CAIR - E,
A
CHRIOST
DEAN
TRO - CAIR - E!

# IRELAND'S CALL

Words and Music by
PHIL COULTER

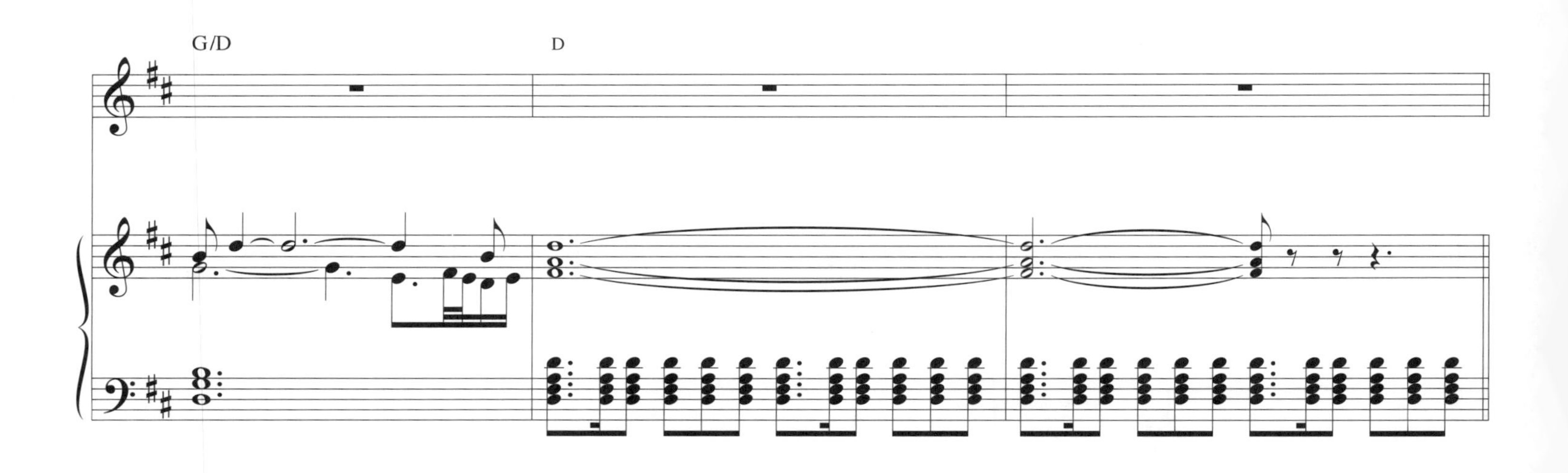


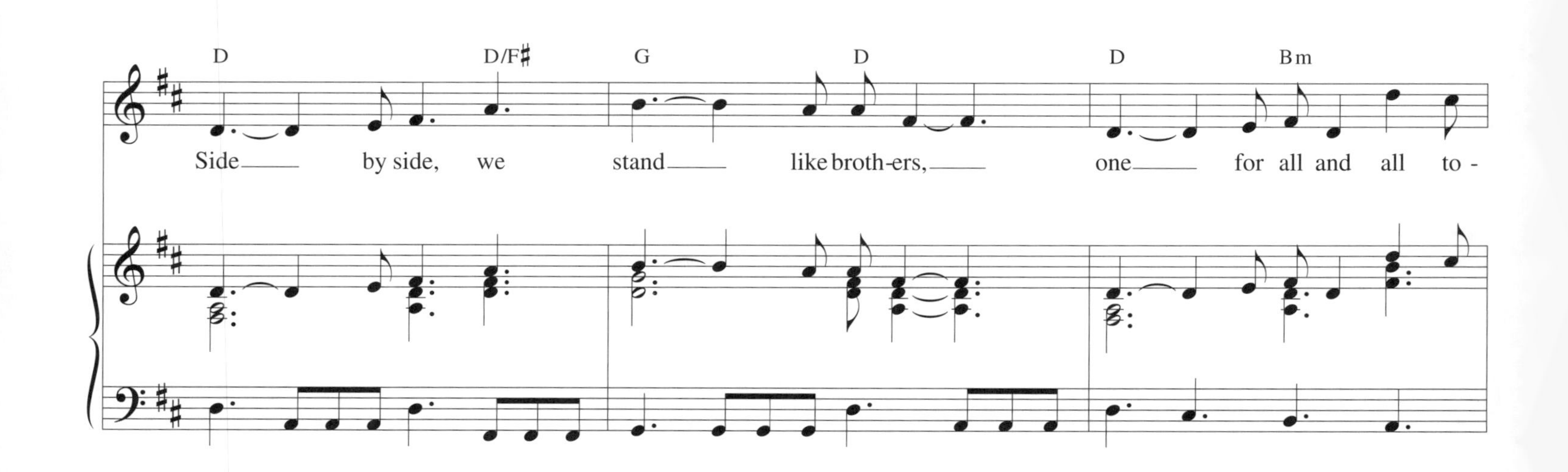

G
A
Bm
G
D/F♯
geth - er: we will stay un - it - ed through dark - er
G
Bm
G
D/A
A
D
G/D
D
A
days and we'll be un - beat - ab - le for ev - er!
D
G
G/B
D
Bm7
IRE - LAND, IRE - LAND!, to - geth - er stand - ing
Asus
A
D
D/F♯
G
tall! Shoul - der to shoul - der, we'll

D/A A D G D
ans-wer Ire - land's call!
D D/F♯ G D D Bm
Come the day and come the hour, some will live in song and
G A Bm G D/F♯
sto - ry. We were born to fol-low our guid - ing
G Bm G D/A A D
star, and to meet our dest-in - y with glo-ry!

Asus
A
IRE - LAND, IRE - LAND!, to - gether stand - ing tall!
D
D/F♯
G
D/A
A
Shoul - der to shoul - der, we'll ans - wer Ire - land's
D
G/D
D
D
D/F♯
call!
Hearts of steel and
G
D
D
Bm
G
A
heads un - bow - ing, vow - ing nev - er to be brok - en, we will

Bm G D/F♯ G
fight until we can fight no more; till our
Bm G D/A D G/D D D G G/B
fin-al requ-i-em is spok-en! IRE - LAND, IRE - LAND!, to-
D Bm7 Asus A D D/F♯ G
geth-er stand-ing tall! Shoul - der to shoul - der, we'll
D/A A7 D
ans-wer Ire - land's call!

B♭7
E♭
IRE - LAND,
A♭
A♭/C
E♭
Cm7
B♭sus
E♭
E♭/G
IRE - LAND!, to-geth-er stand-ing tall! Shoul - der to
A♭
E♭/B♭
B♭7
Cm
A♭
shoul - der, we'll ans-wer Ire - land's call! we'll
E♭/B♭
B♭
E♭
A♭/E♭
E♭
ans-wer Ire - land's call!

# THE ISLAND

Words and Music by
PAUL BRADY

F
Gm/F
F
Gm/F
F
B♭
child - ren dy - in' in the street.
ho - ly flag is gon - na fall!"
And we're still at it in our
Up here we sac - rif - ice our
F/A
C 9
C 7
F
own place, still tryin' to reach the fut - ure thru the past;
child - ren to feed the worn - out dreams of yes - ter - day
still tryin' to
and teach them
B♭
F
carve tom - or - row from our tomb - stone.
dyin' will lead us in - to glo - ry.
But, hey! Don't lis-ten to me!
But, hey! Don't lis-ten to me!
C 7/F
F
B♭(add9)
C 11
C/B♭
This was-n't meant to be no sad song;
This was-n't meant to be no sad song!
we've heard too much of that be -
I've sung too much of that be -

F/C C7 F C7
fore. Right now, I on - ly want to be here with you___ till the
fore. Right now, I on - ly want to be here with you___ till the
B♭/D C7/D Gm/FF C11 F
morn - ing dew___ comes fall - ing.___ I wan - na take you to the
morn - ing dew___ comes fall - ing.___ I wan - na take you to the
B♭(add9) F/C C7
Is - land___ and trace your foot - prints in the sand:
Is - land___ and trace your foot - prints in the sand.
F C7 B♭/D C7/D
and, in the eve - ning, when the sun___ goes down,___ we'll make love___ to the sound of the
And, in the eve - ning, when there's no - one a - round,___ we'll make love___ to the sound of the

1
Gm/F F
2
Gm/F F
oc-ean.
They're rais-in'
oc-ean.
Now, I know us
F Gm/F F Gm/F F Gm/F
plain folks don't_ see all the sto-ry;
and I know this "Peace and Love" 's just cop-pin'
F Gm/F F Gm/F F Gm/F
out.
And I guess these young boys dy - in' in the ditch-es
is just what
F Gm/F F B♭
be-in' free_ is all a-bout:
and how this twist - ed wreck-age down a

F/A
C 9
C 7
F
main street will bring us all tog-eth-er in the end: and we'll go
B♭
B♭maj7
march - ing down the road to free - dom,
free - dom,
free - dom...

# LAUREN & I

By KEITH HARKIN and
PHIL COULTER

B♭(add2)
F
D m
still I can't see you!
And the seas-ons pass aw-ay
and
B♭ma7
D m
I still sit here lone-ly each and ev-'ry day,
wond'-rin' what's gone wrong,
B♭ma7
F
'cos I don't rem-em-ber seas-ons last-ing, oh! so long, oh! so long!
F
C/F
B♭/F
And I still can't see you!
(I'm dream-ing ev'-ry night,

F
C/F
B♭/F
And I still can't see you!
I'm searching ev' - ry day!)
(I have-n't been the same,
F
C/F
B♭/F
B♭/F
N.C.
And I still can't see you!
I'll nev - er sleep a - gain!)
Lau-ren and I,
F
Dm
F
Dm9
Dm
Lau - ren and I!
B♭(add2)
B♭
F
F(add2)
F

F
Dm
And there's the stars way in the sky, leading my way'n I don't know where or
B♭(add2)
F
why; but still I can't see you!
F
Dm
And, when my back's ag - ainst the wall, I see a reas-on for it
B♭(add2)
F
all, still, I can't see you! And I

F
C/F
B♭/F
still can't see you!
(I'm dream-ing ev'-ry night,
And I
I'm search-ing ev'-ry day!)
F
C/F
B♭/F
still can't see you!
(I have-n't been the same,
And I
I'll nev-er sleep a-gain!)
F
still
C/F
B♭/F
can't see you!
B♭/F
N.C.
F
Lau-ren and I,
D m
Lau-ren and
F
I!
D m
Lau-ren and I,
F
D m
Lau-ren and I!
F

# LOVE THEE DEAREST

Music arranged by PHIL COULTER
Italian lyric by MUSKER and KABALLA

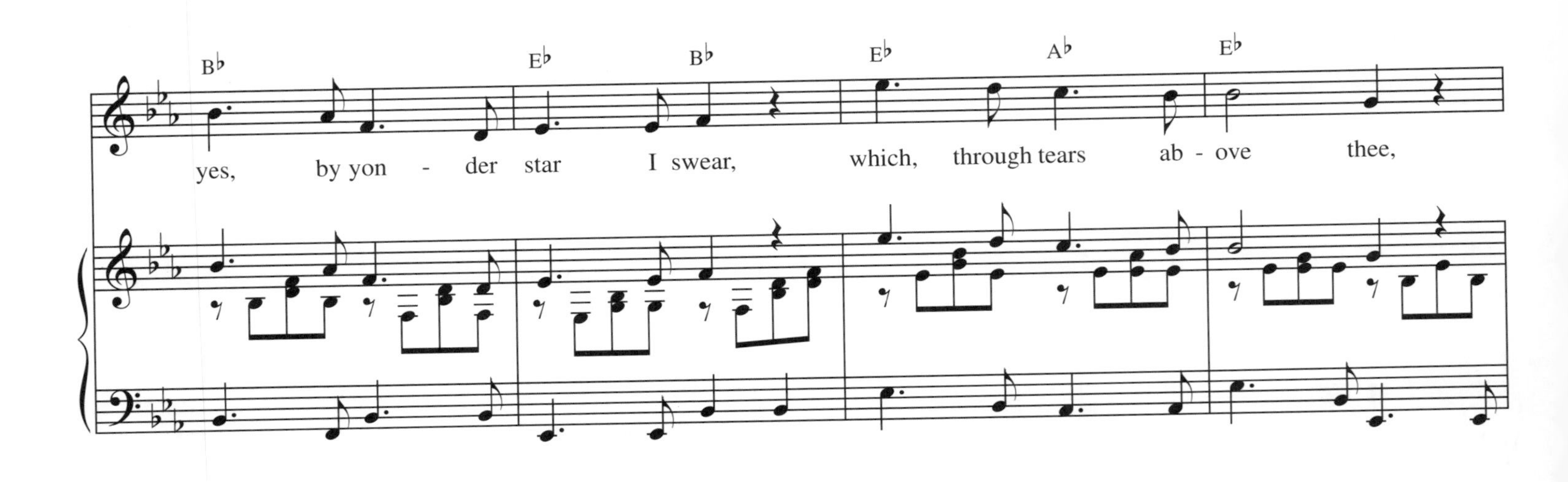

Fm
B♭
A♭/B♭
B♭
E♭
A♭
him my truth will shine!
And love thee, dear - est,
E♭
B♭
E♭
A♭
E♭
love thee: yes, till death, I'm thine!
B♭
B7
E
A
E
Dor - mi a-mo - re, dor - mi!
B
E
B
E
A
E
Por - ta il fuo - re do - ve vuoi.
Vo - la ver - so i sog - ni,

B E B E
bel - la co - me sei. Tue sei per me la stel - la she per
F♯m B A/B B E A
sem - pre brill - er - a; e dor - mi a-mo - re,
E B E E A
dor - mi e gia not-te or-mai. Dim - mi, a-mo - re,
E B E B E A
dim - mi che non te ne and-rai mai piu. Quan - te not-ti in -

E
B
E
B
son - ni se mi man - chi tu?
Ac - cant - o a me le
E
F♯m
B
A/B
B
nu - vo - le non tor - ner - an - no mai,
e
E
A
E
B
A/B
B
sog - na tut - ti i sog - ni che l'am - or - e
C
D
E
da!
L'am - or - e da!

# THE MOUNTAINS OF MOURNE

Arranged by
PHIL COULTER

F7 E♭ B♭/D Cm7 B♭
gangs of them dig - gin' for gold in the street; at
let me rem - ark, with reg - ard to the same, that
F7 B♭ Gm7 F7
least, when I asked them, that's what I was told, so I
if, at those ros - es you vent - ured to sip, the
B♭ B♭ Cm B♭/D E♭ F Cm7 F7
just took a hand at this dig-gin' for gold. But, for
col - ours might all come aw - ay on your lips. So, I'll
B♭ B♭ Cm7 B♭/D E♭ Dm Cm7
all that I found there, I might as well be in the
wait for the dark rose that's wait - ing for me in the

F7
F7
F11
F7
E♭
B♭/D
Cm
B♭
place where the dark Mournes sweep down to the sea!
place where the dark Mournes sweep down to the sea!
E♭
Cm7
F
E♭
B♭/D
Cm7
1
B♭
2
B♭
B♭
E♭
Cm7
There's
F
E♭
B♭/D
Cm7
B♭
B♭
You rem - em-ber young Dav-ey Mc-

E♭ Cm7 F7 E♭ B♭/D Cm7
Lar-an, of course: well, sure, now he's 'round here with the rest of the
B♭ E♭ Cm7
force. I saw him one day as I was cross-ing the Strand, and he
F7 E♭ B♭ F7
stopped the whole street with a wave of his hand! And, as we stood
B♭ Gm7 F7 B♭ B♭ Cm B♭/D
talk - ing of days that are gone, the whole town of Lon - don stood

E♭ F Cm7 F7 B♭ B♭ B♭/D
there to look on! But, for all his great pow- ers, he's
E♭ Dm Cm7 F7 F7 F11 F7 E♭ B♭/D Cm
wish - ful, like me, to be back where the dark Mournes sweep down to the
B♭ Cm F7 B♭ B♭ B♭/D E♭ Dm Cm7
sea. But, for all his great pow- ers, he's wish - ful, like me,
F7 F7 F11 F7 E♭ B♭/D Cm7 B♭
to be back where the dark Mournes sweep down to the sea.
rit.

# MULL OF KINTYRE

Words and Music by PAUL McCARTNEY and DENNY LAINE

C
G
much have I seen, dark dis - tant moun-tains with val - leys of
deer in the glen, car - ry me back to the days I knew
green, vast paint - ed des-erts with sun-sets on fire, as she car -
then: nights when we sang, like a heav-en - ly choir, of the life
C
D
D7
G
- ries me home to the Mull of Kin - tyre.
and the times of the Mull of Kin - tyre.
Bagpipes with voices
E♭
A♭ma7
A♭6
A♭
A♭6
Mull of Kin - tyre

E♭ A♭ma7 A♭6 A♭ A♭6 A♭ E♭
Mull of Kin - tyre Mull of Kin -
tyre.
B♭
Mull of Kin - tyre, oh,
E♭ma7 E♭6 E♭ E♭6 B♭ E♭ma7 E♭6 E♭
mist roll - ing in from the sea, my des - ire is al - ways to
E♭6 E♭ 1 B♭ 2 B♭ Cm7/F B♭
be here, oh, Mull of Kin - tyre. Mull of Kin - tyre.

# MY BOY

Words and Music by CLAUDE FRANCOIS,
JEAN-PIERRE BOURTAYRE, BILL MARTIN
and PHIL COULTER

Em
Dm
Esus
died: this is no hap-py home but God knows how I've tried,
game, tak-en all I can take; but I'll stay just the same
E
Bm7/F♯
E/G♯
Am
Dm
G
be-cause you're all I have, my boy, you are my life, mypride, my
C
F♯m7
B7♭9
B7
joy and, if I stay, I stay be-cause of you, my
Esus
1.
E (no chord)
2.
E (no chord)
boy!

C
C
Sleep on! you have - n't heard a
G/B
Am
E
word; per - haps it's just as well. Why spoil your lit - tle dreams, why put you thru' this
Am
F
hell? Life is no fair - y tale, as, one day, you will
Esus
know but, now, you're just a child; I'll stay here and watch you grow!

E
Bm7/F♯
E/G♯
Am
Dm
Be - cause you're all I have, my boy, you are my
G
C
F♯m7
life, my pride, my joy and, if I stay, I stay be -
B7♭9
B7
Esus
E
F♯m7
E7/G♯
cause of you, my boy! Be - cause you're
Am
Dm
all I have, my boy, you are my
f

G
C
life, my pride, my joy and, if I
F♯m7
B7♭9
B7
stay, I stay be - cause of you, my
E sus
E
Am
boy! My boy!
Dm/A
E/A
A (major)
rit.

# THE OLD MAN

Words and Music by
PHIL COULTER

D
E
A
F♯/A♯
Bm
fath - er, my teach-er, my best friend; and he'll still be heard in the tunes we shared, when I
phea-sant, as she ris - es in the dawn; and how to fish, or make a wish be-
B/D♯
E
F♯m7
E/G♯
F♯m7
E
D
play them on my own. And I nev - er will for-
side a fair - y
A
D
A
D
get him, for he made me what I am: tho' he may be gone, mem-'ries

VERSE 3:
I thought he'd live forever,
He seemed so big and strong!
But the minutes fly and the years roll by
For a father and a son.
And, suddenly, when it happened,
There was so much left unsaid;
No second chance to tell him "Thanks!"
For ev'rything he'd done.

CHORUS:
And I never will forget him *etc.*

# REMEMBER ME, RECUERDAME

Words and Music by
PHIL COULTER

A
D
Bm
com - rade strums on a sad gui - tar; my mind is drift - ing to
E
A/C♯
D6
D(♭5)
D
where you are. I'm hold - ing you as I used to do, rem -
A/E
E7
A
em - ber me, rec - uer - da-me, mi am-or!
D
C♯m
So long a - go, so far away, each

Bm E/G♯ A E/G♯ F♯m
night I pray I pro - mise you that,
C♯m Bm
come what may, those days will stay ev - er in my mem - o -
G E A
ry! In all this world, I could
D Bm E
nev - er find the love that I had to leave be - hind: but

A/C♯
D6
A/E
du - ty calls, so, what - e'er be - falls, rem - em - ber me, rec -
E7
A
uer - da - me, mi am - or!
D
C♯m
Bm
E/G♯
E
Instrumental
A
F♯m
C♯m

Bm
G
C
God only knows what tom-
molto rit.
a tempo
F
Dm
G
orr - ow brings; you're in my heart, so my spi - rit sings and
Em
C
F6
F
C/G
I'll be strong just as long as you rem - em - ber me, rec -
G7
C
uer - da-me, mi am - or!
rit.

# RIDE ON

Words and Music by
JIMMY MacCARTHY

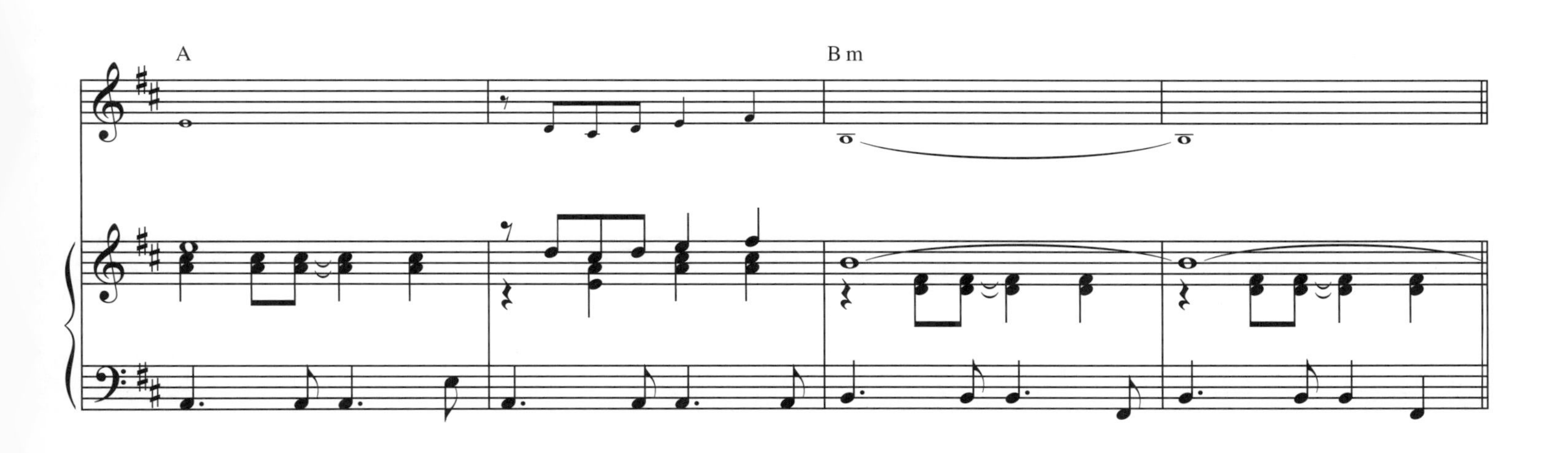

A
Bm
stand - ing six-teen one or two with eyes wild and green.
run your claw a - long my gut one last time. I turn
Bm
G
You ride the horse so well, hands light to the touch:
to face an emp - ty space where you used to lie;
A
I could nev - er go with you, no mat - ter how I
I look for the spark that lights the night through a
Bm
Bm
wan - ted to.
tear - drop in your eye.
Ride on,

G
A
see you!
I could nev-er go with you, no mat-ter how I
B m
B m
wan-ted to!
Ride on,
G
see you!
I could nev-er go with you, no mat-ter how I
B m
1
2
B m
wan-ted to!
(Guitar)

G
A
B m
C m
Ride on,
A♭
B♭
see you!
I could nev - er go
with you, no mat - ter how I wan - ted to!
C m
Ride on,

A♭
B♭
see
you!
I could nev - er
go
with you, no mat - ter how I
C m
wan - ted to!
B♭
I could nev - er
go
with you, no mat - ter how I
C m
wan - ted to!
B♭
I could nev - er
go with you,
no mat - ter how I wan - ted to!
C m

# STEAL AWAY

Written by PHIL COULTER

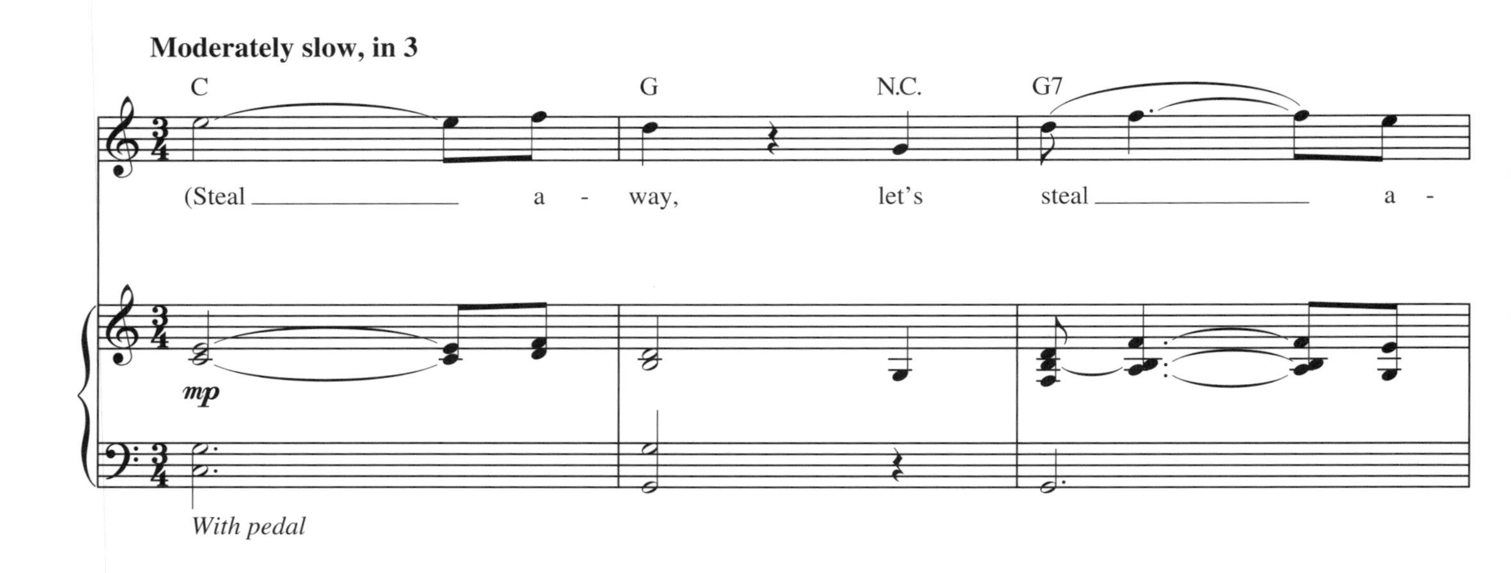

G7
C
C/E
F
F/E
Dm
start a - new and, dar - lin',
G9
To Coda
C
E7sus/B
E7/B
steal a - way. Ooh.)
Let's
We'll
A
E/G♯
E
E7/G♯
A
E/G♯
steal a - way and chase our dream, and
leave with just our mem - o - ries, and
D/F♯
A/E
D(add2)
D
F♯m/B
Esus
Esus2
hope they nev - er find us.
make a new be - gin - ning.

E A E/G♯ E E7/G♯
The drear - y days, the emp - ty
We have to choose to win or
A A/C♯ D(add2) D F♯m/B E E7/G♯
nights, we'll leave them all be -
lose, and it's time we start - ed
1 2
A F/G G G
D.C. al Coda
hind us.
win - ning.
(Mm, ah.) ah.)
CODA
C A♭/C B♭/D E♭
way.)
Steal a -

B♭ B♭7 E♭sus E♭ E♭/G A♭ E♭/G
way, let's steal a - way. No rea - son
Fm7 E♭ B♭/D A♭/C B♭7
left to stay. For
E♭ B♭ B♭7
me and you, let's start a -
E♭sus E♭ E♭/G A♭ Fm7(add4) B♭7 E♭
new and, dar - lin', steal a - way.

# THAT'S A WOMAN

Words and Music by
PHIL COULTER

Fm
Fm Cm7 Fm
del - ic - ate creat - ure is some - thing she ain't, bet - ter take it from me, that's a wom - an; that
Treat her as if you just don't give a damn, that's how to han - dle a wom - an; be
Fm
Fm Cm7 Fm
is - n't an ang - el, that is - n't a saint, bet - ter take it from me, that's a wom - an! She
more of a stall - ion, less of a lamb, that's how to han - dle a wom - an! Keep her
B♭m
B♭m Fm7 B♭m
knows how to please and she knows how to play, take it from me, that's a woman; for -
hang - ing ar - ound till she's read - y to burst, that's how to han - dle a wom - an! Don't
E♭/G
E♭7
get that you hon - our and love and ob - ey, she'll take you and break you and throw you aw - ay, that's a
try to be bad: be the worst! Do un - to oth - ers, but just do it first, to a

A♭
C7
wom - an, that's a wom-an! She
wom - an, to a wom-an! Be
Fm
Fm Cm7 Fm
knows ev - 'ry - thing and she knows ev - 'ry trick, take it from me, that's a wom-an! How to
wise, be wa - ry and be on your guard, that's how to han - dle a wom-an. If you
Fm
Fm Cm7 Fm
kill with a word and cut to the quick, take it from me, that's a wom-an!
feel that you're fall - ing, bet - ter be hard, that's how to han - dle a wom-an. Don't
B♭m
B♭m Fm7 B♭m
How to look through you as if you're not there, take it from me, that's a wom-an;
let her get clos - er and don't let her in, that's how to han - dle a wom-an; 'cos

E♭/G
E♭7
how to say "No" with a flick of her hair, she'll turn you and burn you and not ev - en care, that's a
if you all - ow her get und - er your skin, my friend, it's the end, 'cos you ain't gon - na win with a
A♭
C7
To Coda
F
wom - an, that's a wom - an!
wom - an, with a wom - an!
First man: Faith - ful and
B♭(♭5)
B♭
C7
true, that's a wom - an! Trust - ing in
F6
F
D
you, that's a wom - an! Gen - tle and

D7 D7♭9 D7 Gm sus4 Gm
G7/B
con - stant - ly car - ing,
strong as the
G7 C7 sus4 C7 Gm7 C9 F
love she is shar - ing!
When you look in the
B♭(♭5) B♭ C7
eyes of a wom - an,
and through the dis -
2nd man: ( Look in her eyes? You'll see nothing but lies, she's a woman!)
F6 F D7
guise of a wom - an,
you'll see it all
( Ev'ry one is the same, she's just playing a game, she's a woman!)

D7 D7♭9 D7 Gm sus4 Gm7
there, there's rom - ance in the air, Both men: noth - ing
C7 Gm/F F F D.S. al Coda
else can com - pare, that's ___ a wom - an!
CODA
Fm
Second man: Look at her bo-dy and look at her move, now
(Stage taps)
Fm Cm7 Fm
that's what I call a wom-an! I'm
(Stage taps)

Fm
Fm Cm7 Fm
think - ing now, I've got some-thing to prove, 'cos that's what I call a wom-an!
(Stage taps)
B♭m
All my moves are stall - ing here, I
B♭m Fm7 B♭m
E♭/G
can't get through to this wom - an: the pipes, the pipes are call - ing here, I
E♭7
A♭
think I could be fall - ing here, for this wom-an, for a

C7
F
woman,
First man: Faith - ful and true, that's a
B♭(♭5)
B♭
C7
wom - an!
Trust - ing in
2nd man: (It couldn't be true, she's just playing with you, what a woman!)
F6
F
you, that's a wom - an!
(Trusting in who? You just haven't a clue! What a woman!)
D
D7
D7♭9
D7
Gm sus4
Gm
Gen - tle and con - stant - ly car - ing,
(Just let it be: this one's for me, what a woman!)

G7/B
G7
strong as the love she is
C7sus4
C7
Gm7
C9
F
shar - ing! Both men: When you look in the
B♭(♭5)
B♭
eyes of a wom - an, and
C7
F6
F
through the dis - guise of a wom - an,

D7
D7
D7♭9
D7
you'll see it all there, there's rom -
Gm sus4
C7
ance in the air, noth - ing else can com -
Gm/F
pare, that's a wom -
Second man:
Who would have thought I'd ev - er get caught?
Both men:
WHAT A WOM-AN!

# THE VOYAGE

Words and Music by
Johnny Duhan

F C C G F
erm-ined not to fail; for the heart's trea-sure, tog-eth-er we set
C C G
sail. With no maps to guide us, we
F C Em/B Am Em F
steered our own course; we rode out the storms when the winds were gale
G F G F C
force. We sat out the dold-rums in pat - ience and hope;

G F C
work - ing tog - eth - er, we learned how to cope.
Em Am Em Am Dm7
Life is an oc - ean, love is a boat: in troub - led wat - ers, it
F G F G Em
keeps us a - float! When we start - ed the voyage, there was just me and
Am F G11 C
you: now, gath - ered round us, we have our own crew!

C
G
To - geth - er we're in this rel -
F
C
C
Em/B
Am
Em
F
at - ion - ship; we built it with care to last the whole
G
F
G
F
C
trip. Our true dest - in - at - ion's not marked on an - y chart;
C
G
F
C
we're nav - ig - at - ing for the shores of the heart!

Em
Am
Em
Am
Dm7
Life is an oc - ean, love is a boat: in troub-led wat -
F
G
F
G
- ers, it keeps us a - float! When we start - ed the voyage, there was
Em
Am
Am/G
F
G11
just me and you: now, gath - ered round us, we
C
have our own crew!